Paula D'Arcy

RIVERS OF SORROW, CURRENTS OF HOPE

a PRAYERBOOK *for the* GRIEVING

Foreword by Joyce Rupp

TWENTY THIRD *23rd*
PUBLICATIONS
NEW LONDON, CT 06320
WWW.23RDPUBLICATIONS.COM

PHOTO CREDITS

COVER & PAGE 60: ISTOCKPHOTO.COM/MYCOLA ▪ *PAGE 7:* PHOTOS.COM/ROMAN ANTONOV ▪ *PAGE 8:* PHOTOS.COM/COMSTOCK IMAGES ▪ *PAGE 11:* "STATUE"-FLICKR.COM/PHOTOS/JOELK75 (LICENSE-CC 2.0 ATTRIBUTION) ▪ *PAGE 12:* PHOTOS.COM ▪ *PAGE 15:* PHOTOS.COM/IRENA DEBEVC ▪ *PAGE 16:* "WINDOW 7"-FLICKR.COM/PHOTOS/CALLIOPE (LICENSE-CC 2.0 ATTRIBUTION) ▪ *PAGE 19:* PHOTOS.COM/ DANIEL VAN DE KAMP ▪ *PAGE 20:* "BIG CHAIN"-FLICKR.COM/PHOTOS/BLYZZ (LICENSE-CC 2.0 ATTRIBUTION) ▪ *PAGE 23:* PHOTOS.COM/KATI MOLIN ▪ *PAGE 24:* DESIGNPICS.COM ▪ *PAGE 27:* "FOGGY MORNING"-FLICKR.COM/PHOTOS/QINNANYA (LICENSE-CC 2.0 ATTRIBUTION) ▪ *PAGE 28:* "WEEPING WILLOWS"-FLICKR. COM/PHOTOS/MENDHAK (LICENSE-CC 2.0 ATTRIBUTION) ▪ *PAGE 31:* PHOTOS.COM/PAWEL BRUCZKOWSKI ▪ *PAGE 32:* PHOTOS.COM/DESERTSOLITAIRE ▪ *PAGE 35:* ISTOCKPHOTO.COM/MALERAPASO ▪ *PAGE 36:* PHOTOS.COM/ZSOIT BICZÓ ▪ *PAGE 39:* "BUTTERFLY"-FLICKR.COM/PHOTOS/SITRON_NO (LICENSE-CC 2.0 ATTRIBUTION) ▪ *PAGE 40:* PHOTOS.COM/ZHIGONG ZHANG ▪ *PAGE 43:* "RAYS OF LIGHT"-FLICKR.COM/ PHOTOS/BRAD_HAMMONONDS (LICENSE-CC 2.0 ATTRIBUTION) ▪ *PAGE 44:* PHOTOS.COM/ROMAN SIGAEV ▪ *PAGE 47:* "FENCE SHADOW"-FLICKR.COM/PHOTOS/IVYDAWNED (LICENSE-CC 2.0 ATTRIBUTION) ▪ *PAGE 48:* PHOTOS.COM/HORIYAN ▪ *PAGE 51:* PHOTOS.COM/GALINA CHEREPANOVA ▪ *PAGE 53:* PHOTOS.COM/JUPITER IMAGES ▪ *PAGE 55:* ISTOCKPHOTO.COM/KRAIVUTTINUM ▪ *PAGE 56:* PHOTOS.COM/JUPITER IMAGES ▪ *PAGE 53:* PHOTOS.COM/DON STEVENSON ▪ *PAGE 63:* PHOTOS.COM/JUPITER IMAGES

Twenty-Third Publications

A Division of Bayard

One Montauk Avenue, Suite 200

New London, CT 06320

(860) 437-3012 or (800) 321-0411

www.23rdpublications.com

ISBN 978-1-58595-900-6

Library of Congress Control Number: 2012953103

Printed in the U.S.A.

FOREWORD

Several years ago, Paula D'Arcy and I loaded our backpacks and met in southern Alabama to walk for a week on one of the Underground Railroad routes. Those days of walking were powerful for both of us as we trudged along on the hot, steaming pavement, following the path that slaves desperate for freedom traveled years before us. As we walked under the blazing sun, unsure of where we would find water and food or where we would sleep for the night, we sensed a bit of what it must have been like when the slaves fled for their lives.

As Paula and I began our journey, I did not realize that part of the blessing for me would be in the daily companionship the two of us shared. Paula and I are both naturally reflective women so our walking held a significant amount of comfortable, silent reflection. Our days also allowed for hours of enriching conversation in which we listened to one another speak about our life experiences and how they influenced our personal growth. On one of those days, Paula described the death of her husband and young daughter when their car was struck by a vehicle driven by a drunken person. Paula, three months pregnant with another daughter, was traveling with her family in that ill-fated car. In that disastrous moment her perception of life and her future changed forever.

I often looked at Paula with amazement during those days of walking. I was keenly aware that beside me walked a woman whose tender and compassionate presence embraced many a wounded soul in her travels to lead retreats and in her personal counseling. I marveled at how she had come through such a devastating experience. Paula carries her painful memories with gentleness. But this has not come easily, as the powerful prayers in this book reveal. The numerous aspects of grief contained here are not those gleaned from a clinical textbook. The haunting voice of anguish weaving through these pages flows from the heart of a woman who has known loss at an excruciating level. The prayers come from one who has struggled in the river of suffering. She understands the distressing, emotional response to significant and unexpected loss. She also knows that it is possible to make it to the shoreline of peace.

If you have known loss in any form you will find the river of your own grief reflected here. You will also find a strong current of hope. These prayers hold the potential of bringing you to peace of mind and heart as you move closer to your own peaceful shore.

JOYCE RUPP— SUMMER 2012

PREFACE

When I first experienced the loss of my family, it felt as if someone were standing in front of me saying, "Here is the life being held out to you. Can you take this situation—this sorrow—and find your way?" I was completely disoriented. It felt like I was in a foreign country, unable to speak the language. So I began to pray.

I prayed to find hope and to have endless questions answered. Prayer expressed my fear and my confusion. I prayed because it was all I could do. I asked to be shown the way. Through prayer I found a God I had never known. In time it made my old concept of God seem feeble by comparison. Prayer picked me up and opened me to a radically new understanding of human life. I began to change from the inside out. Eventually, the change freed me.

Why are you so downcast, O my soul?
Why do you sigh within me?

PSALM 43:5

❧

CONFUSION

God, are you there? Are you listening? I blinked my eyes and everything I care about has vanished. How is this possible? And how do I go on?

I cannot bear the sinking feeling that life will never return to normal and things will not work themselves out. This is not a bad dream—it has really happened. What if nothing makes sense again?

How could there be joy and happiness and then, in an instant, my loved ones are gone. Gone where? I cannot draw a full breath. I just want to sleep and not know.

Please answer. I don't need images, I need you. Will you stay with me? Life feels terrifying—the loss, the pain of their deaths, the loneliness (I will never see them again), the confusion, the guilt (I should have been able to prevent this). How do I go on? □

In my distress I called upon the Lord,
to my God I cried for help.

PSALM 18:6

DESPERATION

Please, God, respond. Tell me how life can be so out of control. Why are there only my questions, and no answers? How can you be silent and uncaring, while I'm holding on to sanity by a thread?

I need you to intervene. You should stop speeding cars, and alter hurtful diagnoses. This is the God I want you to be. This is the image I choose. This is what I need, in order to go on: I need you to correct things and protect me.

There are so many decisions to make and I cannot think. I can't take charge. I just stare at the wall. Do you see me?

Are you aware of me and how desperately I am trying to piece things together? Will I ever laugh again, or see beauty? I cannot imagine it. Are you aware that I'm here, drowning? Please, please help me. □

I am poured out like water, and all my bones are out of joint;
my heart is like wax; it is melted within my breast.

PSALM 22:14

WHY?

God, I have to know why. I cannot take another step without knowing why, because if I can't understand what has happened, how can I ever trust you or life again?

The crushing pain in my chest frightens me. What if the pain never eases and this is how I feel for the rest of my life? It feels as if someone has hurled a red-hot brick at me, and it dropped into my heart. I want this to stop but I don't have the power to take the brick away.

I'm scared. Are you listening to me? I will never be "me" again. Now I'm whoever I used to be, plus this heartache. And I'm sitting here weeping because I want the other me back. I want to turn back time but I don't know how, and I'm too exhausted to figure it out.

Help me, please. □

II

My God, my God, why have you forsaken me? Why are you so far from helping me, from the words of my groaning? PSALM 22:1

❧

PAIN

Life should be fair and reasonable. People should die in chronological order and without suffering. And you, God, should protect the good and offer some guarantees.

You are not the God I need you to be. What is the purpose of this life you've created? Tell me, what is the point?

I was a good person who lived peacefully, harming no one. I pursued good things. So then, why me? Why is this sorrow happening to me? Are you somewhere, watching over me? I pray that you are, even though I do not understand you at all.

I don't want to learn to live without them. My daughter will never fall in love—never receive a first kiss. Never bear a child.

Nothing I've known has hurt this deeply. Pain tears through me like a gathering storm. I had big goals and a beautiful dream. Death shatters everything. □

Is it nothing to you, all you who pass by?
Look and see if there is any sorrow like my sorrow…

LAMENTATIONS 1:12

❧

FEAR

God, every part of me cries out for explanations and answers, but there is only mystery. I wrestle with rising fears and endless confusion. What if I never find my way? What if my search for help is pointless?

Maybe love is too great a risk. Who could be persuaded to love if it means knowing this comfortless place?

I used to believe I was in control, but no longer. There's only this utter powerlessness, this experience of life's great no: No, you cannot have the life you wanted, in spite of all your careful plans.

People tell me these events are your will. Is that true? How could I possibly move closer to such a God? What would convince me?

Everyone offers platitudes: Time will heal this. I don't need platitudes. I need truth. My heart is burning for truth. Please, at least let me feel your presence. □

Why, O Lord, do you stand far off?
Why do you hide yourself in times of trouble?

PSALM 10:1

BROKEN DREAMS

The world felt solid and trustworthy until everything I counted on changed. Now I'm painfully aware that life moves. It's the same with my emotions.

Yesterday I was filled with anger, and my fury struck out at you. Why didn't your hand reach out to save everything I loved?

But today I'm begging you not to leave me alone in this darkness. I hate this roller coaster of feelings. I feel splintered. I'm a collection of fragments too small to piece together again.

Grief has robbed me of my dreams. Everything is broken. What do I do with these pieces? Sometimes it takes all my energy just to remain sane. Where are you? Since nothing about life is what I imagined it to be, is it possible that you are nothing like the image I've held of you? I need real answers. □

As a deer longs for flowing streams,
So my soul longs for you, O God.

PSALM 42:1

❧

EMOTIONS

God, I'm praying in order to stay sane. Waves of emotion are moving through me. I hate these storms that come without warning, roaring through my limbs. My mind won't shut off. It races. I feel like all that's left is who I might have been. It's as if I'm alive by default.

Sometimes I still can't believe this has happened. I sit at a red light and think, this really happened to me.

I had a completely different life. I had everything, and then, nothing. And now, this pain, this pressure in my chest. This rootless feeling, as if I'm swimming on the surface of life.

Will I be okay? Please stay with me. When it's this hard, I'm very tempted to think of myself as a victim. I want to stop trying and just let myself be pitied. Can you help me reach instead for my strength and resilience? □

Do not cast me off, do not forsake me,
O God of my salvation! PSALM 27:9

❦

RESISTANCE

God, I cry out even though I question whether or not you are really listening to me. Truth be told, I pray you are there. I can't hang on much longer. Is it something in my nature that makes me resist these losses every step of the way?

Everything seems heavy; I'm growing weary. When I'm overwhelmed, I'm sorely tempted to say that I don't care anymore. But I do.

Maybe my own resistance is what's draining me. I'm very hurt because life seems so unfair. But what if holding myself against the flow of life is making me suffer even more?

I don't want this pain to win. If I give up my version of life and accept life as it is, would my acceptance of their deaths betray my loved ones? That's what I really fear. Do you understand what I'm asking, and how frightened I feel? □

Relieve the troubles of my heart,
and bring me out of my distress.

PSALM 25:17

MEETING PAIN

If I live in opposition to life, am I also living in opposition to you? Can you teach me to live differently? Is there a way to meet pain without closing my heart?

God, it feels like I'm in a crucible. Will I melt or harden?—that's the question. And what do I really want?

Keeping my heart open is such a challenge. It's the hardest thing I've ever tried to do. But what is my alternative? I don't want to run away from this grief and become an embittered old woman. I fear that ending more than I fear this pain.

I'd really like to have been given an easier life. Can you show me how to meet the pain and still be open to love? Could you send me a small sense of peace? I need reassurance that this suffering is not the final say. □

You will roll them up like a cloak,
and like a garment they will be changed.

HEBREWS 1:1

ֵֶּ

CHANGES

God, I will never understand grief. Last week I felt hopeful and I even made progress. This week I don't want to go on. Is this normal? Will grief keep pulling me forward and backward?

Everything is shifting, including my relationship with my loved ones. I can no longer picture them very clearly. I'm forgetting the sound of their voices. What pain this brings. Soon I will know them only through my heart.

I feel like I need a new way to communicate with them. Their spirits are available to me, but their dear bodies are gone. If I lose the memory of their physical presence, are we still connected?

Those people who are telling me to "just move on" never felt these feelings and don't know the anguish. Why doesn't anyone prepare you for this, or teach you how to make the transition? Please, show me. □

My face is red with weeping, and deep darkness is on my eyelids...
JOB 16:16

❧

SADNESS

Today I am weeping for a past I cannot have. I wasn't done with them; I had hardly begun.

God, do you understand my human heart? Life forces me to say goodbye when I had barely said hello. Every day I watch the tide pull the water, the same way death is pulling me. I'm clinging to memories, and longing fills my bones. What will make this end?

What if someone else dies, and I lose even more? My initial shock has become a deep sadness. The fog has retreated. Now I'm face-to-face with the stark reality: They will not return. This is my life.

A friend begs me to acknowledge how difficult this is, and to stop trying to grieve perfectly. Perhaps I cannot see the stress and its magnitude. God, just don't leave. ☐

Heal me, O Lord, and I shall be healed;
save me, and I shall be saved.

JEREMIAH 17:14

❧

HEALING

God, I want to find healing within this suffering. I pray to see what I haven't yet seen. Let me feel you next to me.

I thought my loved ones were all that made life worthwhile. That belief gave them tremendous power. I see that now. I let them become my god, my sole source of happiness and reason for living. How did that happen?

Today I watch sunlight sweep across a weeping willow tree. A willow tree is strong, but flexible. It survives many storms by yielding to the wind.

Now I'm trying to yield to this grief. I make some progress, and then everything unwinds. The pattern repeats. Still, I hope I'm making a little ground. Even though I'm frightened, I'm trying. I want to heal and I want to grow. □

I commune with my heart in the night;
I meditate and search my spirit…

LISTENING

I'm sitting in a chair, listening for you. I want to know you. I want you to hold me like I hold this cup of tea in my hands. Nothing makes sense, but I want you to be with me.

I'm slowly letting go of being so right about things. I know now how much I don't know. Teach me how to let this sorrow change me; I want to find my way.

At first, I was too angry and afraid—the loss was too crushing. I wanted you to change my circumstances. But now I'm simply sitting here, listening.

Help me to see things more clearly. Teach me about the human heart. I'll keep showing up with this teacup. You seem to be at work in life with a totally different purpose than the one I've been insisting upon. Now I'm sincerely trying to listen for your greater knowledge. □

For you have delivered my soul from death, and my feet from
falling, so that I may walk before God in the light of life.

PSALM 56:13

❧

OPENING TO LOVE

God, as I continue to walk the road of grief, I pray you will turn this pain to awareness. My heart is slowly learning what it means to love without possessing, to hold a loved one very lightly. I have always clung to those I love. I avoided thinking about the fact that one day we would say goodbye. If I hadn't been clinging, I might have realized much sooner how precious and fleeting life is, and perhaps made different choices.

I've denied so much about what life really is. Give me new eyes. I'm like a stone you're wearing smooth. Help me surrender the old me so that my soul will open up.

I like these conversations with you. I used to think of you as a remote, distant deity who was demanding. That was my image, but I don't think it's who you really are. □

I will give them one heart and put a new spirit within them.

EZEKIEL 11:19

OPENING THE HEART

Please help me. I want to keep opening my heart. I'm healing at my own pace and in my own way, and yet I share this life/death cycle with all creation.

I'm beginning to look beyond myself. I've focused only on these losses for so long. But many people suffer, and there is so much to think about if I really want to live in the world differently.

My life before this grief was so innocent. I had no idea what heartache felt like, or how strong the waves of grief could be. I had no idea, really, about you. I kept you in a compartment and only thought of you when I wanted something.

I don't know what it feels like to live from a heart that is truly open, and to love from that freedom. But I want to know. Please, transform the old me. □

The people who sat in darkness have seen a great light; and for those who sat in the region and shadow of death, light has dawned.

MATTHEW 4:16

AWARENESS

O God, make my eyes see more each day. I lived with little awareness until this suffering cut through me. It's like a blade that's causing everything false to fall away. It's cutting away darkness and exposing a new light. Am I actually capable of living my life differently, with more honesty?

Maybe the real purpose of life is far beyond these deaths that have shattered my dreams, forcing this unwanted journey.

It's clear that I cannot recapture what I've lost. The question is, will I capture what lies ahead? Perhaps I haven't lost my life's purpose. I only lost that particular purpose.

Is it possible that we are all here to fulfill many purposes and many dreams? This realization is new, and tender. God, help me live more authentically. □

O Lord my God, I cried to you for help,
and you have healed me.

PSALM 30:2

NEW REALIZATIONS

God, I'm beginning to see the beauty in what I've been given. My heart is opening. I want the end result of having loved these dear ones to be the creation of more love in me.

I want the final statement to be love. I want to hand something back to life. I want to be defined by the love we shared, and not by their deaths.

I now see that I did not own them; they weren't mine. The realization forces me to look at my life and decide what to do with it.

Help me, God, because I don't want to stand at this threshold and miss the miracle. I cannot change what has happened, but I can change how I live.

I've believed in you, studied about you, doubted you, even read about the experiences others have had with you. Now, I want to meet you directly. □

Lead me in your truth, and teach me;
for you are the God of my salvation.

PSALM 25:5

WHAT IF?

What if? What if we'd left for our trip on a different day? What if we'd left five minutes later, or three minutes earlier? What if the drunk driver had chosen a different route, or never gotten into his car at all?

What if we'd stayed at home, working in the garden? What if my loved ones' injuries were minor? What if I'd nursed them for years, and then they recovered?

What if all of this was a terrible, terrible dream? But what is, is. This is what I'm beginning to understand. And I pray with everything in me to accept this truth and feel your hand on my shoulder. What is, is.

This is a huge step, to quietly accept what is. I don't want any days of my life to slip by unlived. Help me accept what is, and draw me into your deeper love. □

You are my strength and my shield.
In you my heart trusts and I find help.

PSALM 28:7

❧

KNOWLEDGE

God, I pray to know what is true. I'm struggling to change the way I look at things, and trying to feel hopeful about a life for me beyond grief.

I've finally let go of my insistence that every question be answered. For months I've asked: Where are they? Are they safe? Are they together? I've focused so narrowly on these questions, but I'm slowly learning how to let things be.

Loss is forcing me to look at things in a new way. I'm beginning to trust that your love is at the core of things, but it's a very different love than I imagined.

Your love moves me toward fullness, and asks me to know who I am. When I rest in your love there are inexplicable moments of peace. The love that's comforting me in the midst of pain is now who I know you to be. □

I called on your name, O Lord, from the depths of the pit…You
came near when I called on you; you said, "Fear not."

LAMENTATIONS 3:55.57

LIFE

God, you didn't answer my prayers for a miracle. You didn't intervene and change my circumstances. For a long while you were silent. Now I look at the gift of life. I've never thought about it so directly. What is life? Am I taking it for granted?

This grief is like a searchlight, uncovering hidden things. I didn't get the life I wanted. I've felt forgotten and left out. My heart hasn't been grateful. In losing my loved ones I've felt ripped open. My illusions are shattered. I stumble a lot.

Yet I'm fighting to keep my heart open in spite of the emptiness and the tears. And life is right here, patiently waiting for me to look in its direction.

An awareness arises that life is a gift of great significance, even if the veil covering its beauty and power is sometimes very thick. Show me more, O God. □

Blessed are those who mourn, for they will be comforted.

MATTHEW 5:4

HAPPINESS

God, in the beginning I was discouraged and couldn't find my way. I cried out, wanting you to provide answers and explain everything. I couldn't see that it was I who had to change first.

I used to walk in my neighborhood and make up stories about the people who lived there. It was easy for me to assume their lives were much better than mine. But I was looking in the wrong direction.

Regardless of fortune or misfortune, life itself is still the great gift. This understanding is the piece I've been missing. I no longer look outside of myself to find happiness.

I see that no set of circumstances will make me happy forever. I'll only be happy when I know your life deep within. It's like finding a thread of love in the darkness. □

*My flesh and my heart may fail, but God is the strength
of my heart and my portion forever.*

PSALM 73:26

GIFT

I like greeting you when I awaken. You're the place where I can say anything, even things I'm ashamed to admit. I trust you with feelings I'm afraid no one else will understand.

I've been very unappreciative of all that's been given to me. I was thankful in a general way, but I never woke up grateful that I had another day. Another day. I never woke up thinking that someone else might be looking at me with envy because their own circumstances were worse.

I was too caught up in envy myself. I had no idea what the gift of life was. Now I see that every person I've known and loved, for however long, is pure gift.

I turned to you in earnest because of this pain, begging your help. And you've come to me as if I'd always been faithful. All my gratitude is too small. □

Come to me, all you that are weary and are carrying
heavy burdens, and I will give you rest.

MATTHEW 11:28

INDWELLING GOD

Beauty and laughter continue. People still know joy and are involved in life and celebrations. Will I too rejoin life one day, and honestly care about such things? If I do, will you still be as near as you are now? I don't want to lose this closeness.

Knowing where you are still perplexes me. Are you really out there somewhere, separate from life, looking on from a distance as I was taught? How can that be? It doesn't feel that way.

You are the next breath. There is no distance or separation; you are the deepest part of everything that is. I watched the sea at dawn this morning. Shore birds and gulls made thin patterns on the sand. I heard their screech as they dove into the water for crabs and snails. I anticipate the day before me now, bursting with life and fully alive. □

So teach us to count our days that we may gain a wise heart.

PSALM 90:12

RESOLVE

Why have I fought what is so fiercely, not just now, but all of my life? Did I want control? Did the illusion of being in charge make me feel less afraid? Why wasn't I able to see that living in this way did not bring peace?

God, lead me to a deeper understanding. Loss has made me feel as if my life is cut and pasted into small pieces. The pieces say: I do not like this; I'm exhausted from trying; I cannot make sense of anything.

Many persons tell me, "You'll never get over this." But there is something more than all these pieces. You are showing me that.

There is the immensity and power of life, a force mysterious beyond measure. I pray that the new opening in my heart will widen. I pray for the resolve to always stop and listen to all that is. □

So you have pain now; but I will see you again, and your hearts will rejoice, and no one will take your joy from you.

JOHN 16:22

❦

SURRENDER

God, in this time of grief the natural world speaks to me powerfully. Today I was drawn to a rose bud that's been sitting in a vase on my table. As her petals slowly softened and fell apart, my own heart opened.

I was struck with a sudden awareness that life in the form of the rose had reached out to me, and something within me reached back in full recognition. The small flower is just one expression of your radiant love which holds all life in being. I accepted her touch and the greater wideness she offers.

I've stopped clinging to my loved ones through memories of the past. Instead, I'm learning to open myself to the power of the love we shared. Surrendering to this, I seem to be gaining things I didn't imagine. Love flows like an inner river, regardless of what's happening on the surface. □

So we do not lose heart. Even though our outer nature is wasting away, our inner nature is being renewed day by day.

2 CORINTHIANS 4:16

TRANSFORMING PAIN

Grief has been all encompassing and at times I've felt unable to go on. I've been like a small boat tossed by high waves on a restless sea. But now there are moments that are not filled with grief, and these become more frequent.

I'm slowly integrating a new awareness: You are the boat and the sea, the wind that's kept me on course. For so long others told me to keep busy and get on with my life. They had no idea. Trying to accept these deaths and sort things out is my life.

If I push the pain aside, it will never be transformed. And this is what I want. I want you to help me transform this pain until my eyes fully open.

In the underworld of grief, I've worked through layers of sadness. Your subtle touch upon my heart is greater than any loss. □

For it is for you, O Lord, that I wait; it is you,
O Lord my God, who will answer.

PSALM 38:15

❧

LONGING

I now trust that all will be well. I wasn't a trusting person before this heartache broke me open. I've held tightly to my own ideas and images of life, asking you to agree with me and make things happen. I thought that was prayer.

I've railed against you (and life) when things didn't go my way. I had no sense, at first, of a larger life and deeper meaning. I had no sense of a power and purpose in life itself. I was living out my life from such a small perspective.

Now I sense a purpose in life much greater than my own story. My inmost longing is to realize everything that this experience has to offer. What do I trust? I trust the force of love. I have hope. For a long while I saw no light at the end of the tunnel. Now I do. □

Even though I walk through the darkest valley,
I fear no evil; for you are with me.

PSALM 23:4

NOT ALONE

Your love rises up in the ground of my being. I bow before this love which has been with me in my sorrow, and was there all along. You've shown me the powerful, loving Spirit that lies deep within. Now I must respond to its presence. It's up to me.

I'm taking small steps forward. I focus less on what I've lost and more on the life right before me. I've made a list of the things that matter in life, and I'm challenging myself to know them. I see that if all I hold onto is pain, I'll miss the powerful love. I want to walk away with love.

Behind all heartache is your Spirit, which exceeds everything. You're not a symbol. You're real. I finally consent to your love, which is capable of changing the heart of the world. □

Surely goodness and mercy shall follow me all the days of my life,
and I shall dwell in the house of the Lord my whole life long.

PSALM 23:6

FREEDOM

God, I've spent months consumed by these losses. I've felt despair and bewilderment. Often I didn't think I could go on, but I did. I didn't think I'd see beauty again, but I have.

This awareness and the new opening in my heart are a silent revolution inside me. I've learned that the depths of pain and the depths of joy come from the same well: life.

Having tasted so deeply of loss, I now see life in a way that wasn't possible before. I see the way we all struggle to find healing and a sense of freedom. In the end there was nothing to find; your love and the path of healing were always within me, waiting.

When the doctor said, "Your daughter and husband have died," you were already in motion, but no answers were spoon-fed. I needed to come toward you with my whole life. □